Questions and Answers on Moral Education

By Kevin Ryan

Library of Congress Catalog Card Number: 81-80011
ISBN 0-87367-153-8
Copyright © 1981 by the Phi Delta Kappa Educational Foundation
Bloomington, Indiana

This fastback is sponsored by the Broward County Florida Chapter of Phi Delta Kappa through a generous contribution from Miss Bessie Gabbard, a member of the chapter.

TABLE OF CONTENTS

Introduction 7

Questions of Definition 9

Moral Education: Pro and Con 13

Approaches to Moral Education 15
   Values Clarification 16
   Cognitive Moral Development 19
   Moral Reasoning 24
   Set of Values 26

A Synthesis Approach 31

Selected Bibliography in Moral Education 38

Introduction

Moral education is again generating attention in both the popular press and the educational literature. It is one of those topics whose importance seems only to be outshone by its complexities that run the gamut from issues of theory to problems of application in schools and classrooms. And like most really important questions, it does not lend itself to easy formulas or quick answers. The purpose of this fastback is to lay bare the major issues of theory and public policy and to suggest how educators might approach their roles as moral educators in the real world of schools.

Before getting to those issues something needs to be said about the term "moral education" and how it is to be used in this fastback. Many people are put off by the term. For some, it connotes repressive actions or puritanical attitudes. For others, it immediately sets up a we-they controversy: "Will we teach our morality or theirs?" While it might satisfy some to use a less loaded term such as "civil education," this is merely a cosmetic effect. The issues residing beneath the term do touch deeply felt attitudes, values, and beliefs; but there is little to be gained from hiding behind a new term. Also, the term "moral education" has a substantial history, and a change of terms would cut us off from that rich history.

Another problem with the term "moral education" is that it has many different meanings. Even meanings of the word "education" vary from conditioning individuals to make new responses to stimuli to introducing people to the best of what civilization has to offer. So too, the word "moral" has meanings ranging all the way from what someone decides feels good in a particular situation to what God has revealed to be good and correct. While it may not eliminate the ambiguities, in this fastback I shall use moral education to mean what the school does, directly and indirectly, to affect both the students' ethical behavior and their capacity to think about issues of right and wrong.

In order to explore the issues and problems surrounding moral education, I have used a question-and-answer format cast as an interview.

Questions of Definition

Q: Could I begin by asking a few questions about your definition? For instance, what do you mean by "What the school does, directly and indirectly. . . . ?"

A: Fine. I mean by those words the things that are consciously or unconsciously done by teachers and administrators in the course of a day or a school year, from ordering textbooks to holding examinations, from counseling troubled children to dealing with disgruntled parents. Some of the things we educators do—some of our interventions in the lives of children—are direct and planned and conscious. For instance, a conscious decision is made that the fifth graders in a particular school will have twenty minutes of outdoor exercise at midmorning every day, weather permitting. That, like other curricular decisions, is a direct intervention. The children get fresh air, run around and get large muscle exercise, and come back ready to refocus on academic tasks. On the playground, though, a handful of boys regularly bully Randy to the point that he fears recess and dreads coming to school. This bullying and Randy's reaction is an unplanned, unconscious, and indirect curricular effect. Consider another example: A high school history teacher believes that students learn more if she involves them in debates over interpretations of particular historical events. In order to do this she typically divides the classes into two debate teams, boys against girls. The direct, conscious interventions lead to learning historical facts and interpretations; also, some skills in how to debate. The indirect and unconscious intervention reinforces the idea that males and females are adversaries which perpetuates the so-called war between the sexes.

Q: What about the other part of the definition—"affect ethical behavior and capacity to think about issues of right and wrong?"

A: This refers to the school's role in clarifying what is ethical behavior. For instance, bullying, lying, or cheating will not be tolerated. On the other hand, promptness, carefully done work, and fairness in dealings among people is stressed. As to thinking, the schools assist in all kinds of thinking—from mathematical to intuitive. The everyday human interaction in schools and the content of the many curriculum areas offer situations through which teachers and students quite naturally confront issues of what is morally correct and incorrect. And, again, with both thinking and behavior, there are things the school consciously and unconsciously teaches, consciously through the overt curriculum and unconsciously through the covert or hidden curriculum. My suspicion is that the hidden, moral curriculum of the school is very strong indeed.

Q: Is moral education just another fad, something else to keep everyone's mind off the school's essential task of promoting learning?

A: I couldn't disagree more! Nothing could be further from a fad. Moral education has been a responsibility of the schools from their beginning. The great Greek philosophers like Socrates, Plato, and Aristotle were all concerned with moral education and devoted much attention to it. The great educational thinkers like Quintilian, Comenius, and Pestalozzi saw the moral development of children as an integral part of the school's role. The nineteenth-century English philosopher, Herbert Spencer, believed the central goal of education to be the formation of high moral character. In our own country such educational reformers as Horace Mann and John Dewey saw teachers and schools as crucial to the moral education of youth and the moral health of the society. There have been some things done under the banner of moral education that have been faddish, but that is nothing new. In the last few years there has been a "back to the basics" movement. Without getting into just what people mean by "basics" and whether or not that is a faddish movement, let me ask you, What could be more *basic* for education than to help children grapple with issues of right and wrong and help them become ethical, socially responsible individuals?

Q: All right, it is not a fad. But is it legal? Can a teacher or a school system engage in moral education without worrying about being hauled into court?

A: For what it is worth, I think the fact that school people are being sued with such frequency is a real indication of the breakdown of trust. We don't know how to deal with controversy reasonably in a face-to-face way, so we run to the lawyers to make sure our own self-interest is served or that we are protected against someone else's self-interest. But let me get back to your question.

A few years ago a researcher, Nicholas Sanders, looked at all the state education charters and state codes he could get his hands on and examined them for references to moral education or the teaching of values and the skills of citizenship. He found support for moral education in 40 of the 44 codes he was able to obtain. The words were different from state to state, but the intentions were quite clear: The schools are expected to promote moral thinking and behavior. On the other hand, there seems to be little in the state codes to suggest that the schools should not consciously try to be a moral force in the lives of students. As with everything else, though, the rights of the individual have to be respected and schools cannot do such foolish things as promote racial intolerance or some other anti-social, undemocratic behavior.

By the way, the founders of our country clearly saw the necessity for moral education in the schools to insure a democratic state. Writing in 1778 about an educational plan for his home state of Virginia, Thomas Jefferson said such a plan "would have raised the mass of people to the high ground of moral responsibility necessary to their own safety and orderly government." John Adams wrote, "Religion, morality and knowledge being necessary to good government and the happiness of mankind, schools and means of legislation shall forever be encouraged by the states." In general, the Founding Fathers perceived public education as central to their noble experiment because they envisioned the school's role as fostering a moral perception of social affairs.

Q: All right, but what about today? These are new times. Is there any support for moral education in the schools today?

A: There seems to be fairly clear evidence that there is support. In 1980, the Gallup poll of public attitudes toward education published in the *Phi Delta Kappan* indicated that 79% of the American people favored school instruction that would deal with morals and moral behavior. This is exactly the same percentage in favor of the school taking an active role in moral education five years earlier when the same question was asked. In that same year, I did a survey of Phi Delta Kappa's own membership and found that 88% of the educators responding expressed the view that the schools should be actively involved in moral education. These are, to me, impressively high percentages of Americans to agree on anything, particularly something that is alleged to be so controversial.

Moral Education: Pro and Con

Q: In your view—which I take it is for the school's being involved—what are the best reasons *for* and *against* moral education in the schools?

A: There is clearly a case on each side. And you are correct, I am in favor of the school being involved.

Let's start with the case *against*. First, morals and values are often very personal. There is too much diversity—diversity that must be respected—to have a program of moral education in our schools. Some groups or individuals would be offended. Second, moral education would be difficult to do without indoctrinating. Teaching what is good and bad is rarely a rational process. The older generation imposes views and values on the young. Schools should not be engaged in indoctrination. Third, morals and values are very complex. Are teachers to decide for society what children should do and think in this area? They have no special training or expertise in these matters. Fourth, if the schools take on and do a poor job of it, there will be a terrific reaction against it. All of the enemies of the schools will come out of the woodwork, and the support that does exist will be eroded further. It would simply be asking for trouble.

That's the case for the opposition.

Now, let me make the case *for* and, along the way, speak to some of the points raised above. First, this is not something new. As I tried to indicate earlier, the schools have always been looked to as one source of moral education. Sure, much of this area is murky and there are many questions unanswered, but that is quite simply the way things are in this arena of life. That is not a valid reason to avoid moral education.

Second, the need for moral education exists and parents and teachers recognize it. I could—and so could you—provide a long list of youth-related problems from drug and alcohol abuse to the high rate of teenage suicides to sexual promiscuity. Although many people are convinced that youth are more morally at sea than ever before, I cannot say that I know this with any surety. I do believe, though, that young people are confronted with many more morally ambiguous problems than earlier generations, and they have less and less support in understanding and resolving them. The family as a teaching unit is weak. So is the church. Television teaches a great deal, and there are real questions as to its impact on the moral thinking and behavior of children, who clearly are growing up in a different world. A few years ago economic historian Robert Heilbroner wrote a book titled *On the Human Prospect* in which he reviews all of the probable catastrophes confronting society—from the probability of our becoming involved in a nuclear war to our chances of surviving without doing serious damage to the ecosystem. Heilbroner concludes that what really has people upset is their inability to pass on their values—presumably cherished values—to their young. Something seems to have seriously impaired the process that worked in the past.

Third, there are things that teachers have always done that have a positive moral effect on children. Also, there are some newer approaches to moral growth and development which I will outline later. But neither of these requires teachers to be trained as moral philosophers or to be certified as saints.

Fourth, whether a teacher or a school is to be involved in moral education is not a matter of choice. Moral education is inevitable. But *how* one teaches moral education is a choice. What is taught or allowed to happen is also a choice. Let me put it this way: You cannot send six-year-old children to school for six hours a day, for 180 days a year for 12 or 13 years, involve them in all sorts of interpersonal situations from classroom to playground, expose them to the history and literature of the human race and not affect them morally. Education is not a value-free activity. Issues of personal and social values and morality are woven into the very fabric of school. The question should be *how* to do it.

Approaches to Moral Education

Q: Could we go then to ways teachers can consciously engage in moral education? Or, as you call it the "how" of moral education?

A: Fine. One way to answer the "how" question is the "three E's" approach and another is to look at some of the alternatives currently being practiced.

Q: Three E's?

A: Yes, that stands for *Exhortation, Example,* and *Experience*—three ways children are morally educated in our schools and throughout the world, for that matter. The first E, *Exhortation*, refers to people telling children what is right and wrong, urging them to behave in this way and not in that way and, in general, instructing them to live by a certain set of standards. A good deal of this goes on in our schools. Sometimes it is subtle exhortation; sometimes it is not so subtle.

The second E, *Example*, refers to the moral or ethical model provided by the teachers or, for that matter, other students. In psychology we refer to this as learning by modeling. The student sees a certain type of behavior—both words and actions—and imitates. For instance, a student sees an example of emotional control when a classmate is quite rude to the teacher who responds firmly but with clear respect for the offending student. The teacher is modeling a certain way of responding to conflict. If the student has a positive regard for the teacher, there is a higher probability that he will respond in like manner in a similar situation than if he has little regard for the teacher. Of course, long before psychology came up with the term "modeling behavior," we spoke of this as the power of good example. While it is an old truth, it is easy for many of us to forget that whether we are teaching long division, or geography, or keeping order in the lunchroom, we are modeling all sorts of other things for children, and prime among them is moral behavior.

But let me move on to the third E, *Experience*, which refers to those situations that involve students actively in experiences where they re-respond with ethical or moral behavior. There are different types of moral experience. For instance, the student becomes involved in a debate about the American use of the atomic bomb on Japan in World War II. Here the experience is primarily intellectual or verbal. Or another example: Suppose the teacher asks the students to give up their Saturday mornings to pick up the debris around the playground. The students are in a very different experience involving both mind and body. They are doing things with moral content, rather than just talking about what is right or correct. I would like to come back to this particular type of experience. Meanwhile, I hope it is clear that each of these approaches can be directed by selfish as well as positive motives—an example can be a bad example; an experience can teach students not to trust others and to look out for "number one."

But let's move on. Another way to look at moral education is to examine some of the actual approaches available to teachers and schools. Let me suggest four approaches currently being used that deserve study and comparison. They are values clarification, cognitive moral development, value analysis, and teaching a set of values.

Values Clarification

The first, and by far the most popular of these approaches is called values clarification. Some key figures in the development of this approach are the late Louis Raths, Sidney Simon, Merrill Harmin, and Howard Kirschenbaum to name just a few. The meaning of values clarification is in the term. The student is given the opportunity to grapple with issues of personal preference, and to discover or clarify what he or she believes or holds dear. Some of these issues relate to personal preferences, for example, the use of leisure time; but many deal with deeper ethical issues, such as one's attitude toward certain crimes, matters of personal conduct, or what one believes constitutes the good life. Through values clarification activities students bring their own values to the surface, and they also hear what other students believe.

Values clarification uses a seven-step scale of valuing from simply making a preferential choice to actually acting on one's choice in a consistent way. In effect, the scale suggests that our values should not exist at just the verbal level, but should be acted upon in our regular life.

In the last fifteen years advocates of values clarification have been very active in developing classroom simulations and games and in holding workshops and conferences for teachers. The classroom materials, which are widely available and easy to use, are designed to help students become aware of where they stand on particular questions of value. For instance, a teacher might ask a class, "What would you do if you suddenly received a surprise gift of $100? Would you put it in the bank? Give it to charity? Spend it on yourself?" Then the teacher goes around the room giving each student an opportunity to respond or to say "pass" if he or she prefers. Values clarification is not supposed to be coercive in any way. In that same vein, the teachers are expected to be quite open and accepting of student responses. Teachers may give their own views, but should do so in a manner that is not authoritarian. But back to the $100.

The teacher may record the frequency of each choice after going around the room and ask for comment on how to interpret the tally. Or, the teacher might change the rules and say, "Now, let's suppose you were given the surprise $100 and you *must* spend it on yourself, on something you want. Okay, what would you choose?" Typically the teacher accepts the students' answers, not probing for justifications of choices or in any way putting students on the defensive.

Essentially, the values clarification approach attempts to get students engaged in a process of choosing, prizing, and acting on their currently held values. The forced choice scheme described above is just one of many methods employed. Among the many others are the value continuum strategy, the value sheets strategy, and the public interview.

In the value continuum exercise the teacher draws a line on the board to represent ranges of opinion on a controversial topic. The ends of the line represent the extreme positions. For instance, the teacher might want the students to wrestle with the question, "What is your position on gun control?" At the left hand of the continuum would be the statement "complete control" and the right hand of the continuum the statement "no control." The teacher indicates that between these two ends there are numerous other positions, and she asks individual students to indicate where on the continuum their views lie. The students are asked to briefly describe their positions without giving their reasons for holding the positions.

In the values sheets strategy students are given a written statement outlining a particular value that might, for example, deal with civil liberties or certain social policies. Students are asked to write their own responses to these statements. Occasionally, the teacher uses the event for class discussion, but the major emphasis is on having the students think through and write their own value statements.

With the public interview strategy the teacher lists a number of topics on the board such as family life, money, sports, politics, boy/girl relationships, and smorgasbord (meaning a wide ranging discussion). The teacher asks for volunteers to be interviewed on a topic of their own choosing. Once there is a volunteer, the teacher engages the student in a public interview. The teacher may ask any question, but the student is free to pass on any question he feels is too personal or doesn't wish to answer. However, if he does answer a particular question, this gives him the right to ask the same question of the teacher. This opportunity to "pass" and the opportunity to ask any question you have answered provides a useful check on invasions of privacy when using the public interview strategy. These are just a few of the many strategies that the values clarification people have developed over the last several years.

Values clarification advocates have made lavish claims about the efficacy of this process. According to some enthusiasts, a values clarification program is supposed to cure tendencies toward apathy, flightiness, uncertainty, inconsistency, drifting, over conformity, over dissenting, and role playing. Conversely it is supposed to help youth become positive, purposeful, enthusiastic, proud, and consistent. There have been a number of evaluations of values clarification programs, and most serious researchers do not believe these claims are upheld empirically.

Still the popularity of the approach with the teaching profession is positive evaluation evidence of a sort. Teachers believe it allows them to deal with important issues in a non-doctrinaire way. They can motivate students to think about issues, but as teachers they do not have to take responsibility for dealing fully with the complexities of each issue. They feel they have done their job by getting young people to confront these value questions and by indicating to them that they believe the confrontation is important.

Values clarification is not without its critics, however. Some critics are disturbed with the values clarification approach because it does not make a distinction between moral and non-moral values. A student's preference for leisure time activities—not usually a moral issue—gets jumbled together with preference on issues of interpersonal fairness and social justice and on such problems as entrenched poverty, euthanasia, and genetic manipulation. Others feel it is immensely superficial, often involving students in heady issues without careful use of the head. Said another way, students express their opinions on moral issues and listen to the opinions of others. Often, however, the essential moral issues are not subjected to thoughtful analysis with careful scrutiny of evidence, examination of the lessons of history, or the testimony of experts. So the student may end up, on the one hand, with the idea that important moral issues do not need to be subjected to careful and thoughtful analysis and, on the other, that his or her opinion on a moral issue is just as good as anybody else's.

Still, it is a movement with a great deal of appeal to teachers and students and, as such, it should be understood by people involved with moral education. While it is surrounded by uncertainties and potential hazards, in the hands of a thoughtful teacher I suspect it has great positive value, particularly if it is not the only approach used.

Cognitive Moral Development

Q: I have read recently about the work in moral education of Harvard psychologist Lawrence Kohlberg. Are you familiar with it?

A: Yes. Kohlberg is the central figure in the second approach called cognitive moral development education, which is said to have implications for schooling.

Since cognitive moral development education is such an unwieldy name, let's simply call it moral development. However, we need to keep sight of the fact that it is a theory that deals with cognitive development and is concerned with *how* we think—that is, the structure of thinking—rather than *what* we think or what we do.

While values clarification was developed by educators and is rather light on theory, moral development has come to us from theory building and psychological research. Only in recent years has there been an attempt to apply it to the classroom. The key individual associated with the theory of moral development is Lawrence Kohlberg of Harvard University. Kohlberg became fascinated by the early work in this area by the late Swiss psychologist Jean Piaget. Piaget, at one point in his life, became interested in how moral judgment develops and how children acquire rules. One of his "experiments" was to get on his knees and play marbles in his village square with young boys of different ages from 5 to 14. While playing with them, he asked them questions about the rules of playing marbles: Where do the rules come from? Can they be changed? What happens if rules are broken? What Piaget noticed—and what became the basic insight upon which Kohlberg has built his theory—is that children at different ages have distinctly different ways of thinking about moral questions. The structure of their thought has certain characteristics but changes over time, becoming increasingly more complex as it considers more aspects of the situation. Kohlberg's research, which has been going on now for almost 30 years, has led to a theory that describes distinctive stages of moral thinking and how people move—and do not move—through these stages.

Kohlberg's theory has been undergoing change over the years, but in its most well-known form he describes six stages of moral thinking. The first stage, which children enter about age three, is the punishment and reward orientation. The child reasons morally on the basis of being rewarded for being good or being punished for being bad. Stage 2 is called the instrumental-relativist orientation. The person thinks about moral issues from a rather selfish perspective and is dominated by the pleasure principle. What is right or fair is what satisfies me or possibly someone close to me. Stage 3 is called the good boy-nice girl orientation. What the majority opinion is or what is the stereotypic view is the correct way. Here we try to live by and live up to the expectations of those around us. Stage 4 is sometimes called the "law and order" orientation. Authority and respect for the social order become dominant here; so does an appreciation of the law as a preserver of the social good. Stage 5 is the social contract and individual rights stage. Moral responsibility is seen from the perspective of a social contract such as the Bill of Rights which states concern for the rights of the individual and concern that the procedures of due process are followed. Finally, at stage 6 is the universal ethical principle orientation, which is, by the way, a stage that few people seem to attain. An individual at this stage habitually reasons according to his or her own conscience, according to self chosen principles such as justice and respect for the dignity of all human beings.

Q: Can you tell what stage I'm at?

A: Everybody wants to know that as soon as they come across this theory. I really have no idea. In order to know, you would have to be tested. Kohlberg has an interview method of determining the stage of an individual. He presents you with a series of moral dilemmas and assigns a stage after examining the structure of your answers. It is not the decision you come to when dealing with the dilemma, but the way you solve it, the sophistication of your thought, that determines your stage of moral development. Other researchers, such as James Rest and John Gibbs, have developed paper-and-pencil tests using dilemmas, that do not require time-consuming interviews.

The technique of using moral dilemmas is very important to Kohlberg and his followers. Not only is it the means by which one's stage is determined, but it is also an important means of helping persons move to higher stages. For moral development to take place, one set of thinking structures must be replaced by another. This is not done, according to Kohlberg, by direct teaching, good will, or good behavior. It results from cognitive clash, from the confrontation of lower stage thinking with higher stage thinking; not just any higher stage, but the thinking of the stage immediately above. If there is a discussion of a moral dilemma in a fourth-grade class, most of the students are probably at stage 2, the instrumental relativist orientation or pleasure principle stage; a few are at stage 3, the good boy-nice girl stage. With the proper interaction the stage 2 children will be attracted to the stage 3 way of thinking. On the other hand, progress is slow and many people get fixated at low levels. There are plenty of adults running around at stages 1 and 2. The majority, though, are at stages 3 and 4. But this cognitive clash, which is so important for forward progress, is also sequential. One cannot jump from stage 2 to stage 4, in effect skipping stage 3. We have to work our way slowly and laboriously through each stage. Also, not all cognitive clash at each stage is effective. Going back to our fourth grade, if the teacher is stage 4 and continually involves herself in classroom dilemmas and other moral discussion employing her stage 4 structures, she will be helpful to the few stage 3 students who would be attracted to her way of thinking, but she would be of no help to the others. Her stage-4 thinking would make no impression on the stage-2 students. They would hear the words but would not comprehend the moral structures. It seems to me that this is why so much moral preaching—at home, in school, and in church—has not been as effective as it might be. There has been too much of a mismatch of stages between the teacher and the learner.

The heart, then, of the cognitive development approach directs educators to confront children with moral dilemmas—problems that have two, or possibly three defensible solutions. The most famous of Kohlberg's dilemmas is the Heinz case, which goes as follows:

> In Europe, a woman was near death from a special kind of cancer. There was one drug that the doctors thought might save her. It was a form of radium that a druggist in the same town had recently discovered. The drug was expensive to make, but the druggist was charging ten times what the drug cost him to make. He paid $200 for the radium and charged $2,000 for a small dose of the drug. The sick woman's husband, Heinz, went to everyone he knew to borrow the money, but he could only get together about $1,000, which is half of what it cost. He told the druggist that his wife was dying, and asked him to sell the drug cheaper or let him pay later. But the druggist said, "No, I discovered the drug and I'm going

to make money from it." So Heinz gets desperate and considers breaking into the man's store to steal the drug for his wife.

The following questions are the kind the teacher uses to reveal the nature of the students' thinking:

1. Should Heinz steal the drug? Why or why not?

2. If Heinz doesn't love his wife, should he steal the drug for her? Why or why not?

3. Suppose the person who is dying is not his wife but a stranger. Should Heinz steal the drug for a stranger? Why or why not?

4. Suppose it's a pet animal he loves. Should Heinz steal to save the pet animal? Why or why not?

5. Why should people do everything they can to save another's life, anyway?

6. It is against the law for Heinz to steal. Does that make it morally wrong? Why or why not?

7. Why should people generally do everything they can to avoid breaking the law, anyway?

8. How does this relate to Heinz's case?

After an initial presentation of the dilemma and some brief discussion, the teacher divides the class into groups based on their solution to the dilemma and then asks each group to come up with its best—most morally strong—reason. Once the groups have done that, a structured debate takes place focusing on the question, "What is the right thing to do and why?"

The purpose of having students grapple with dilemmas is to aid them in developing more complex reasoning patterns. Usually the dilemmas are tailored to fit the experiential level of the students. By continual exposure to the intellectual tension and higher stage thinking, children acquire higher and more comprehensive stages of moral reasoning. Kohlberg justifies the schools teaching this process by insisting that the U.S. Constitution is a stage-5 document, and to insure the future of our democracy we must help children reach this level. While it's an interesting point, it is odd that teaching children higher levels of thought—moral and otherwise—needs justifying.

Kohlberg's theory of moral development is an optimistic one. We do indeed progress naturally, but there are definite things educators can do to foster growth, and to assist the natural process. Once we reach a particular level, there is no backsliding. As Kohlberg's theory and associated research have become better known, and since he and others have attempted to apply it to schools, a number of practical and theoretical questions have been raised, only a few of which I will mention.

First the theory is continually being modified, and reputable research journals have published reports raising questions about the empirical basis for the theory and the positive results of programs where this approach has been applied. Second, the theory is a rather narrow one, concentrating as it does on reasoning and only indirectly affecting behavior. It is questionable whether American parents are going to buy an approach to moral education that concentrates exclusively on thinking and has so little to say about how children actually behave. My own concern is the turning of this whole issue of moral education into a word game with few implications for action. Teaching our children how to discourse about complex personal and social issues without helping them in the world of action could be an empty and dangerous victory. This particular criticism, by the way, holds true for values clarification, too.

Still, Kohlberg's work appears to be of basic significance. It follows alongside a great deal of other research that suggests we go through definable and distinct physical and psychological stages. It may very well be that it is much too early to judge the potential of this approach to moral education for schooling.

Moral Reasoning

Q: Very interesting. But I'd still like to know what stage I'm at.

A: Believe me, so would I. But since I can't tell you that, let me tell you about the third approach instead. The third approach is called moral reasoning. Actually, it goes by many names, such as skills for ethical action, value analysis, cognitivist approach, teaching philosophy to children, and strategies for solving values questions.

This approach has an old and honored tradition. Quite simply, teachers instruct children in a process of solving moral problems. They are not trying to give children answers but a way of proceeding when confronted by problem issues. They try to equip them with logical thinking skills so they don't have to rely on emotional response or prejudices. Advocates of this moral reasoning approach believe children should be able to provide reasons why stealing should not be permitted. Further, they should be able to determine under what circumstances a particular act of stealing might be justified. They should be able to answer such questions as: Is there such a thing as a just war, and if so, under what conditions?

Advocates of moral reasoning argue that it is essential for individuals in a society to solve moral problems rationally and to be able to understand and interpret the nation's Constitution and other founding documents. While the arguments are similar to Kohlberg's cognitive moral development approach, the supporters of moral reasoning see important differences. Specifically, they believe in equipping the child with reasoning skills for analyzing ethical decisions rather than setting up situations (discussions of dilemmas, for instance) and hoping that the transition to higher moral stages will eventually take place. Such an approach is both too arbitrary and too passive for the proponents of moral reasoning. While they object to the cognitive moral development approach, they often have disdain for the values clarification approach, which they believe is anti-rational and ultimately bases important human decisions on personal preferences and one's affective responses. Instead, they recommend that the schools teach a process of moral reasoning.

There are a number of moral reasoning schemes, many of which come directly from philosophical ethics. One such system has been advanced by Jack Fraenkel. It involves seven steps. The first is to identify the dilemma. Second, identify the alternatives. Third, predict the consequences of each alternative. Fourth, predict the short- and long-term consequences. Fifth, collect the consequential evidence. Sixth, assess the correctness of each consequence according to a number of criteria based on the enhancement or diminution of human dignity. Seventh, decide on a course of action.

Students practice each of these steps using games and learning aids until they are proficient with the whole strategy. Advocates are quick to point out that much of the curriculum content from literature to biology is replete with issues and events that can be cast into problem form. This is particularly true of the social sciences and history, and many scholars in these areas have been leaders in developing this moral reasoning approach.

As attractive as this approach is and as old as its tradition, moral reasoning is not widely practiced. One obvious reason is that relatively few teachers have taken courses in ethics; many are unable to articulate their method of moral problem solving, and until this condition is remedied, the approach will have very limited application. Another objection raised is what is seen to be its excessive rationality and disregard for the emotional side of moral decision making and behavior. Are we to believe these are areas where the affective has no place at all?

In summary, although this third approach, moral reasoning, has a long history in education, particularly at the college level, there are a number of interesting efforts to adapt the approach for elementary and secondary school students. However, definite proof of the wide-scale effectiveness of value analysis is yet to come. But, to answer your question about your personal stages of moral development, an advocate for moral reasoning would say, "Don't worry about the stage where you are. Make sure you have the ability to think through ethical issues. Make sure you have a defensible *process* of moral reasoning."

Set of Values

Q: All right, then. I think I have a sense of what's involved in teaching moral reasoning. How about alternative four?

A: Here the school sets out to teach a particular set of values such as courage, respect for property, and fairness in dealings with others. Like moral reasoning, it is a very old approach. Certainly in our country right up to World War II educators were comfortable with this approach, and it was the rule rather than the exception. Although some schools had explicit values they taught, values that were sometimes written on the facade of the schools or in the hallways (e.g., "Virtue is its own reward" or "Knowledge, Service and Love"), in most cases the values were implicit. Commonly accepted values were love of learning; respect for hard work and achievement; desirability of certain personal habits such as courage, kindness, and self respect; and certain social attributes such as respect for property and settling differences in a nonviolent manner. These represented what many educators believed was the subtle curriculum of the school. Basic skills were important, but so were these values. Indeed, some argue that their values were the primary curriculum.

These values were taught in a variety of ways by being modeled by the teachers, by announcing them to the children, by building them into the rules, regulations, and expectations for how students should behave, and often by embedding them in the curriculum content itself. For instance, fairness was a behavior teachers tried to reflect. It was clearly a behavioral expectation and was often the subject of readings and discussions in such subjects as history and English. I suspect that the effectiveness of this approach to teaching a particular set of values is dependent upon the setting in which students are exposed to these values. In other words, the value milieu is the message.

Q: This alternative seems different from the first three?

A: In what way?

Q: Well, for one thing the others all have particular practices associated with them, but doesn't this approach to values seem much more pervasive?

A: I agree, but it is an approach we have not researched as much as the others. For example, the value of fairness; it is only one of the values to be taught, and traditionally we have used the three E's—exhortation, example, and experience. It would be difficult to identify those factors or incidents that cause a student to acquire the value of fairness. Besides the problem of distinguishing what values are learned in school or elsewhere, there is the problem of identifying what within the school environment specifically contributed to the acquisition of the value.

Put simply, different students learn in different ways. Some learn through verbal instruction, some by modeling, some through what teachers and other students expect of them, and some through various combinations of all of these. This alternative seems to allow for many different student learning and teacher instructional styles.

Q: If a school were to institute this approach, where would the set of values come from?

A: Good question! In most cases values have evolved over time and are not always clearly articulated. They represent what the majority of the people believe is important and right. The distinguished anthropologist, Claude Levi Strauss said:

> I do not believe that any society can be built upon a purely rational foundation. Men, to live together, need something more, a set of values which are beyond dispute and which are the living link among them.

That is part of the answer, then. The values come from the beliefs and expectations of the people.

Another source of values is founding documents, like our Constitution and Bill of Rights. We believe in life, liberty, and the pursuit of happiness. These values are reflected in school. However, since not all communities have the same values, not all schools have the same values. One would expect the people in a small Portuguese-American fishing village in Rhode Island to have different values than the citizens of Beverly Hills, California. And in a democracy like our own, with locally controlled school systems, we would expect the schools to reflect some of these differences in the values that are promoted.

We have just come through a period where our values have been under severe pressure. First, since World War II there have been many changes in our society, often resulting in stress and strain on the value system. Then the Vietnam War divided people into hawks (who valued patriotism, standing by our allies, and respect for elected officials) and doves (who valued peace, non-violent methods of settling disputes, and dissent against rigid authority). Add to this the civil rights struggle, the sexual revolution, and Watergate and it is clear why people felt that as a society we had no common set of values to pass on to our youth. Then someone came along and claimed there was a generation gap—with different values held by young and old. There was even a slogan, "Don't trust anyone over 30." I am oversimplifying the point, but in this environment people were confused about *everyone else's* values and concerned about what values the schools were passing on.

Teachers seemed to be just as divided over value issues as everyone else, and they became unsure about their role as value transmitters. Without a clear sense of a shared value system and a common morality uniting us, it seems to me that schools took a less aggressive role in value transmission. In my opinion, much of the reported current career dissatisfaction of teachers and the widespread problems of discipline in schools are closely related to teachers surrendering some of their role as interpreters and supporters of the community's values. Further, I suspect that what is lurking behind the vaguely defined back-to-the-basics movement is more than a concern for reading, writing, and arithmetic. Many people sense the school's uncertainty and loss of moral authority and teachers' seeming willingness to put up with unruly behavior from students. In an inarticulate way, the public is sending the schools a message. Whether that message is being heard or not, is unclear. But it is being communicated by refusal to support bond issues and tax levies for schools.

Earlier I mentioned the Gallup polls in which 79% were in favor of instruction in the schools that dealt with morals and moral behavior. It seems to me that this particular approach of teaching a set of positive social values supports this community desire. My colleague Andrew Oldenquist calls this approach directive moral education. It enables the school both to instruct certain values and to set behavioral standards. For instance, if a school is clearly committed to teaching respect for the rights of others and service to the community as necessary attributes of a good citizen, then the faculty will stress these values through direct instruction, through the school environment (sometimes called the hidden curriculum) and through expected standards of behavior. It also means the schools provide experiences in the normal flow of activity where children can be involved in activities which demonstrate these values.

Q: What is the case against this fourth alternative?

A: This set-of-values approach has its critics. Some, like Kohlberg, say it cannot be done. He describes the set-of-values position as the "bag of virtues" approach, where the school pulls certain virtues out of the bag and tries to teach them. Kohlberg believes that such an approach has no psychological validity. Others object to the pedagogical approach, because they consider it indoctrination. The methods appear to involve manipulation of children. Although not necessarily so, the appeal is to the emotional, the unreflective, the non-rational.

A third objection centers around the question, "Just whose set of values are we going to teach?" If ours is a pluralistic society, respectful of the values of all groups, can the public schools support one set of values without seeming to favor one group and to offend the other? This is seen as all right for private schools and religious schools, but not for the public schools.

These, then, are the arguments pro and con on alternative approaches to moral education that are typically presented to teachers and educational administrators.

A Synthesis Approach

Q: I think I understand these four alternatives, but I am curious about where you stand. And what would you do if you were running a school?

A: Let me answer both of those questions, but one at a time. Realize that I am stating my preference. First, I do not think it is a matter of choosing one of these alternatives and rejecting the others. I do not see them in opposition to each other. Each approach has certain strengths and should be used to gain certain ends. Values clarification should be used to bring values issues and problems to the fore and for motivational purposes, but it should not be expected to be the entire moral education of school children, which I believe is the case presently in many schools. The same is true of the other alternatives. So often in education, there has been a search for the "one right way," but I believe people living in a free and democratic society are just too complex to be well served by one approach. Another way of saying this is that people have different learning styles. Furthermore, these different approaches stress different aspects of moral thinking. Since individuals are interested in or need different things at different times in their lives, this suggests to me that we should draw on all of these alternatives.

Second, I believe the fourth approach, that is, directly teaching a set of values, needs to be reemphasized. Let me quickly state the reasons for my support, because this approach is most frequently attacked by advocates of the other three approaches. Foremost among the reasons is my belief that Americans are bound together by a common set of values. These values are stated in our Constitution, our Bill of Rights, and our laws. Further, they are embedded in our traditions and the daily lives of our citizens. Some of these values are respect for the rights of others, for fairness, for cooperation, for competition and the pursuit of excellence, for compassion for the underdog and the oppressed, for courage, and for hard work. I can see nothing anti-democratic or offensive to any particular religious or ethnic group if the school consciously tries to promote such values as these. On the other hand, failure to promote them could be social suicide or, at the least, it could mean having to live in a society very different from the one we have now. I am quite satisfied that the schools are justified in promoting what have been seen as positive American values. And, I am sure the courts would see it that way, too.

With regard to the issue of indoctrination, we run into some semantic problems. In our society, indoctrination has a negative connotation. It conjures up visions of weird religious sects and fanatical political groups. But some kinds of indoctrination go on in our schools starting with kindergarten. A. S. Neill, the founder of the famous Summerhill school, abhorred indoctrination, but there was clearly indoctrination going on in his school. For me, it comes down to a matter of degree and method in particular situations. For instance, to attempt to instill patriotism largely through heroic stories of current leaders, martial music, and frightening scenarios of what will happen to us if we don't give blind obedience to those in authority is clearly objectionable, if not downright dangerous for a democratic society. Yes, there is a place for songs and for honoring our heroes through stories, but teachers also need to make a case for patriotism, or any other value for that matter, by using moral reasoning.

Schools are involved in moral education whether they want to be or not; in some fashion they impose a set of values on students. Some schools and teachers are more direct and more conscious of the values they are imposing, but by the very nature of education, all do it. What I believe is that first, these values be identified publicly and then be sensibly woven into the fabric of school life.

Let me now turn to what I believe is the most serious deficiency of all four of these alternatives. I began our conversation by defining moral education as what the schools do directly and indirectly to affect both the students' ethical behavior and the way they think about issues of right and wrong. If you think back over these alternatives you will notice that they seem to deal very heavily with thinking—helping children intellectually clarify their values; getting them to function at higher levels of moral thinking; teaching them a way to think through a moral problem. In recent years, the behavioral end—what children and young people actually do—has been all but absent from the American discussion of moral education. While I believe the intellectual dimension is immensely important and should be the primary focus of the school's efforts; nevertheless, how our children behave is of ultimate importance to parents, to the children themselves, and to the society. Being able to talk a good game is not, and should not, be the aim of a school's moral education program. As teachers and administrators we want children to learn to behave as good citizens, good parents, and good individuals. We want students to know their values and to act on them, to think on high levels but also to act on high levels.

Let me give one example of a behavioral aspect of moral education, which has to do with being a contributing member of society. A persistent theme among many young people is "I feel useless. I am no good to anyone." If a child does not excel in school as a student or an athlete, he or she may have very low self-esteem. In our technologically sophisticated society, the opportunities are few for children to be of help, to make a meaningful contribution to others. There are few farms and family businesses where youth can learn to work and to contribute. Add to this the child-centered quality of American homes and schools, and we end up with children who have a good deal of practice receiving but very little giving. If you examine it, the only game in town for most children is school. And if all school does by way of moral education is talk about what is right or wrong, then we should not be surprised if our children are self-centered and incapable of giving to others.

Q: Okay, that's the problem. But what is the solution?

A: A long time ago Aristotle was asked, "How does a man become virtuous?" and he responded that a man becomes virtuous by doing virtuous acts. He becomes brave by doing brave acts. He becomes kind by doing kind acts. People need opportunities to learn value-related skills and opportunities to put values into operation. We do not become brave or courageous simply by talking about it or reading about brave deeds. This may help, but people need practice. Well, let's go back to the school's role in helping children to become contributing members of society. I think a case could be made that, while we still value helping others as a goal, the opportunities for children to learn how to contribute and to get practice are increasingly limited in the schools and in the community.

What I am suggesting is that parents, teachers, and the total community build back into the lives of children chances to contribute to others and to get practice helping. Schools can and should lead the way here. First, they can set the clear expectation that children within this particular school are expected to help others. Second, teachers can instruct children in simple skills of helping. Third, they can make opportunities available for children to get practice at helping. Here I believe we should start early by having children take responsibility for keeping the classroom neat and orderly, but gradually children should be given chances to help one another. Children tutoring other children is one example. Older children helping lower grade teachers with an individualized reading and spelling program is another. There are many tasks that children can do, from correcting papers to helping keep the school library operating at top efficiency. Ultimately children must have chances to help outside the school. Schools should act as brokers between individuals and institutions needing help. A little imagination and energy will turn up innumerable opportunities, from shut-ins who need errands to be run and a friendly face with whom to talk to day-care centers that have a continuing need for volunteers to give individual attention to young children. There are blind people who need to be read to and helped in numerous ways. There are increasing numbers of elderly people living apart from their families on marginal incomes who need help. There are also class projects, such as keeping a small park litter free. But these first three steps are not enough.

Children and young adults need opportunities to reflect on and talk over their helping experiences. Teachers have a very important role here in helping students solve problems and get perspectives on what they are doing. But, basically, the helping experiences carry intrinsic value themselves and the learning is in the doing. Schools should not just help children think and talk about moral issues, but should go a step further and make opportunities for students to *act* morally.

Q: So I take it that if you were running a school, you would institute a program of moral action?

A: That would certainly be a strong recommendation I would make. But let me go back and sketch what I would do to promote the development of moral education. First, I would hold consciousness raising and informational meetings on moral education for both teachers and parents. It is important to keep parents informed all the way along the line. Informed, they will be your biggest supporters; uninformed, they could destroy your best efforts.

Once there is support from the parents and teachers in the community and a decision is made to go ahead, then we move into the second phase, the study phase. There is more than sufficient literature on this topic. Groups should study all four of the alternatives, not with a view toward choosing the one they prefer, but with the intention of integrating approaches and then adapting the integrated approach to the local scene. Earlier I gave examples of activities that stress the helping relationship, but if a community wished to stress other values, appropriate activities could be built into the overall approach. It is really a matter of deciding what values a community wishes to stress and then addressing them through the curriculum and through the learning climate of the school.

An important part of this study phase involves a self study of the school—which attempts to gauge its moral climate by the activities currently going on and by the signs of trouble, such as a high level of vandalism or absenteeism.

The third step is organizing the program itself. Whatever is done should be of local design. However, the program should have certain general characteristics. For one thing, it should be public. Parents and other teachers should know what will take place at specific grade levels or within particular subject matter areas. There should be no mysteries about what is being taught. The program should be integrated and coordinated. Each teacher should not be encouraged, willy-nilly, to use A, B, and C values clarification games; M, N, and O moral dilemma discussions; or X, Y, and Z moral reasoning skills. While avoiding a lock-step curriculum, there should be some structure to moral education similar to the structure in students' scientific education. The program should not stress just the verbal; there should be an experiential dimension.

The fourth and final step is program evaluation. As in all aspects of schooling, we should try to ascertain the impact of what we do. At this stage there are no highly developed evaluation techniques for moral education. There are some common-sense approaches, such as checking to see if there have been any changes in the rates of vandalism and absenteeism. Another source of evaluative feedback comes from teachers. Do they see the program making a difference with students in their classrooms? A survey of teacher attitudes and observations could be an important source of data. In addition, there are instruments which measure the level of moral development. One instrument developed by James Rest of The University of Minnesota and one by John Gibbs of The Ohio State University use short, paper-and-pencil formats. These could be used both for diagnostic and program monitoring purposes.

These four steps, then—consciousness raising and information sharing with teachers and parents, a study program leading to a general plan, the development of a detailed curriculum and implementation plan, and finally, a system of evaluation—are what I believe to be broad parameters of a program of moral education.

Q: One last question, and it's a question of opinion, not fact. Today, educators are being told what we should be doing from ecology to drug education. What do you think will happen if we just ignore moral education?

A: Keep in mind that moral education goes on whether we consciously address it or not. Our children and young people are continually getting an education in values and morality—from television and the rest of popular culture, from peer groups, from their families, and from what goes on in school. What I am suggesting is that we try to do the job more deliberately and constructively, that we plan what we do. We do this with science and physical education. Why not moral education?

Q: But, what will happen if we don't take this matter seriously?

A: Frankly, I don't know. I'm sure we could both recite statistics to one another about the rise in the rate of teenage suicides, drug addiction, sexual promiscuity, and vandalism; but I really don't know what those figures mean. Instead, let me conclude by switching roles with you and asking you some questions for which you ought to have answers: Do you think our schools are helping to develop people with values you admire, people you feel confident can preserve our way of life? Are you happy with what the schools are currently doing? If not, what are you going to do about it?

Selected Bibliography in Moral Education

Dewey, John. *Moral Principles in Education.* New York: Philosophical Library, 1959.

Fraenkel, Jack R. *How to Teach About Values.* Englewood Cliffs, N.J.: Prentice Hall, 1977.

Gibbs, J. C.; Widman, K. S.; Colby, A. "The Sociomoral Reflection Measure," in Kahmerker, K.; Mentkawski, M.; and Erickson, V. L. *Evaluating Moral Development and Evaluating Education Programs That Have a Value Dimension.* Schenectady, N.Y.: Character Research Press, 1980, p. 101-112.

Hersh, Richard H.; Paolitta, Diana P.; and Reimer, Joseph. *Promoting Moral Growth: From Piaget to Kohlberg.* New York: Longman, 1979.

Purpel, David, and Ryan, Kevin, eds. *Moral Education: It Comes with the Territory.* Berkeley, Calif.: McCutchan Publishing Corporation, 1976.

Raths, Louis E.; Harmin, Merrill; and Simon, Sidney. *Values and Teaching.* 2d ed. Columbus, Ohio: Charles E. Merrill, 1978.

Rest, J. R. "New Approaches to the Assessment of Moral Judgement," in Lickeona, Thomas, ed. *Moral Development and Moral Behavior: Theory, Research, and Social Issues.* New York: Holt, Rinehart, and Winston, 1976, p. 198-218.